NOTEBOOK

RULED PAPER

THIS BOOK BELONGS TO:

authored by: Marcel Doll, Hammerschbüchel 10, 53797 Lohmar, Germany

Made in the USA
Monee, IL
10 December 2021

84683405R00068